The Library of SPIDERS™

Trap-Door Spiders

JAKE MILLER

The Rosen Publishing Group's
PowerKids Press™
New York

Published in 2004 by The Rosen Publishing Group, Inc.
29 East 21st Street, New York, NY 10010

First Edition

Editor: Jannell Khu
Book Design: Emily Muschinske
Layout Design: Eric DePalo
Photo Research: Emily Muschinske

Photo Credits: Cover and p. 1 © James P. Rowan; pp. 5, 14 © Anthony Bannister, Gallo Images/CORBIS; pp. 6, 9, 10 © Robert and Linda Mitchell; p.11 © Eric De Palo; pp. 13, 17, 18, © Peter J. Bryandt; p. 21 (top) © Michael & Patricia Fogden/CORBIS; p. 21 (bottom) © Karen Tweedy-Holmes/CORBIS.

Miller, Jake, 1969–
Trap-door spiders / Jake Miller.
    v. cm. — (The Library of spiders)
Includes bibliographical references (p.   ).
Contents: Trapdoor spiders — The trapdoor spiders' family — A trapdoor spider's body — Built for digging — The trapdoor spider's tunnel — How trapdoor spiders hunt — Trapdoor spider eggs — Baby trapdoor spiders — The trapdoor spider's enemies — Trapdoor spiders and people.

ISBN 0-8239-6710-7 (lib. bdg.)
1. Trap-door spiders–Juvenile literature. [1. Trap-door spiders.] I. Title. II. Series.
QL458.4 .M55 2004
595.4'4—dc21

                              2002014771

Manufactured in the United States of America

Contents

Trap-Door Spiders

Trap-door spiders dig tunnels under ground and line the tunnel walls with their silk. They also make a doorlike opening at the top from silk and dirt. These spiders spend most of their time in their tunnels with the doors closed. They hide from their enemies and their **prey**. Female trap-doors even raise their young in their tunnels. If they haven't caught prey in a while, trap-door spiders are forced to leave their tunnels to find food. Male trap-door spiders also leave their tunnels when it's time to **mate**. Young trap-doors build their homes extralarge, so that they can still fit inside when they are fully grown.

This trap-door spider has opened the door of its tunnel home. The spider will close the tunnel door before leaving. The door hides the tunnel entrance from enemies and prey.

The Trap-Door Spider's Family

Trap-door spiders belong to the Ctenizidae **family** of spiders. This family has some of the oldest **species** of spiders on Earth. This means that spiders in the Ctenizidae family are very similar to spiders that lived millions of years ago! Members of the Ctenizidae family have special rakelike teeth that they use to dig their tunnel homes.

Many trap-door spiders make their homes in the tough soil found on sunny hillsides throughout countries where it is warm. In the United States, trap-door spiders can be found across the south from Virginia to California. Although they may look scary, trap-door spiders are not harmful to human beings.

Trap-door spiders live in warm areas of the world. (Top) This rare cyclocosmia trap-door spider lives in southeastern United States. (Bottom) A brightly colored red trap-door spider lives in Tanzania, a country in Africa.

The Trap-Door Spider's Body

Spiders have two main body parts. A spider's head is called the **cephalothorax**. This is where the **fangs**, mouth, eight legs, and eight eyes are attached. Two of the eyes are in the center and three are on each side. The cephalothorax is also where the **glands** are located that produce the **venom** spiders use to kill their prey. The second main body part of a spider is called the **abdomen**. Trap-door spiders use their **spinnerets**, located on the abdomen, to spin silk for their tunnels. Most trap-door spiders have a dark brown cephalothorax and legs, and a gray or tan abdomen.

This is a close-up shot of a trap-door spider. Notice its fangs. Female trap-door spiders are about 1 ⅜ inches (33 mm) long. Males have thinner bodies, and only grow to be about 1 inch (25.4 mm) long.

fangs

Born to Dig

Trap-door spiders are different from other kinds of spiders. Most spiders have fangs that work sideways, like pinching fingers. The fangs of trap-door spiders point straight down, like the big teeth of a walrus. Trap-door spiders use their jaws to dig their tunnels. Their jaws have spiny rakes which help to break up dirt. They roll loose dirt into a ball and then kick it out of the hole using their back legs. Trap-door spiders in North America dig tunnels that are up to 1 inch (25.4 mm) wide and 12 inches (30.5 cm) deep. Some kinds of trap-door spiders dig tunnels that are almost 2 feet (61 cm) deep.

(Left) Notice the eight eyes and the jaw located on this trap-door spider's cephalothorax. These spiders use their powerful jaws to dig their tunnels.

(Right) This is a drawing of a trap-door spider's jaws. Trap-door spiders use the spiny rakes on top of their jaws to dig into the ground to make their tunnel homes.

rake

The Trap-Door Spider's Tunnel

Each trap-door spider species builds its tunnel in its own special way. Some species make tunnels that are a single tube using only one entrance. Other species make several entrances to their tunnel. Some species make thin doors with only silk and a little dirt. Other species use sticks and other scraps to make thicker lids. The outside of the door is **camouflaged** so that the entrance is hard to see. Some trap-door spiders also spin fine threads around the trapdoor to make a sort of alarm system. When an insect touches the silk, the spider feels the threads move.

(Right) With the tunnel door closed, this trap-door spider can safely hide from most of its enemies and prey.

(Below) The inside of this tunnel door is lined completely with silk. The entire tunnel is also lined with silk.

tunnel door

tunnel

How Trap-Door Spiders Hunt

The trap-door spider hunts at night, after waiting safely inside the tunnel all day. Early in the evening, the trap-door spider will open its door and stick out its front legs. It waits at the entrance until it sees prey walk by. Or it may feel something touch one of the silk alarm threads. The spider will quickly jump out and shoot venom into its prey with its fangs. The venom kills the prey. The trap-door spider drags its prey back into the tunnel to eat it in safety.

Trap-door spiders eat insects such as ants. Some species of trap-door spiders even hunt small lizards and birds! After they have eaten, some trap-door spiders leave the remains of their prey at the bottom of the tunnel. However, other trap-door species will roll the remains into a ball and push them out the trapdoor.

When an insect passes near this trap-door spider's tunnel, the spider will quickly attack and drag the prey inside its tunnel home. Trap-door spiders build their tunnels in areas where there is plenty of prey.

Finding a Mate

Female trap-door spiders rarely leave their tunnels. Because of this, male trap-door spiders must search for females when it is time to mate. The males follow the smell of the females' **pheromones** and search for their trapdoors. When a male finds a female's trapdoor, he checks the pattern of silk to make sure that the female is of his own species. The male will then show off to the female by drumming his legs. If the female recognizes this dance, she lets the male mate with her.

Female trap-door spiders lay their eggs in a silk eggsac near the tunnel walls. An egg sac can contain up to 300 eggs.

eggs and
spiderlings

Baby Trap-Door Spiders

Baby spiders are called spiderlings. When trap-door spider eggs hatch, the spiderlings share the tunnel with their mother for a few weeks. In some species of trap-door spiders, the young stay with their mother for up to eight months. The spiderlings look like tiny copies of their mother. When they are ready to build their own trapdoor tunnels, the young leave their mother's tunnel. Many of them leave by ballooning. This means they each spin a strand of silk and stand in the wind. The wind picks up the silk and carries the spider away. The silk acts as a kite, using the wind to carry the spiders through the air. The wind may carry them just a little way or many miles (km) away. When they land, the spiders find the best places to dig their tunnel homes. Depending on their species, trap-door spiders live from one to two years.

These are baby trap-door spiders on the bottom of their tunnel nest. When they are ready to leave, they will leave by ballooning. Ballooning spiders have been found as high as 5,000 feet (1,524 m) in the air!

The Trap-Door Spider's Enemies

A trap-door spider's best **defense** against **predators** is its tunnel, where it hides from danger. To keep an enemy from entering, the trap-door spider will grab the door with its fangs and hold on to the walls of the tunnel with its legs. Most predators give up and go away. Some wasps that hunt spiders don't give up so easily. A wasp can slice through the trapdoor with its sharp jaws to get inside. It will quickly **paralyze** the spider. The wasp then lays eggs inside the spider's body. When the eggs hatch, the baby wasps eat the spider from the inside out.

(Left) Birds, lizards, spiders, and insects, such as wasps, are predators of trap-door spiders. This wasp is stinging a spider. Although the spider is not dead, the venom in the sting has paralyzed the spider so that it can't fight back or run away.

(Right) The best defense a trap-door spider has is to hide inside its tunnel home. This spider is closing its trapdoor to keep away predators. Notice how the outside of the trapdoor looks exactly like the rest of the area. When the door is completely closed, it is difficult for predators to see the trapdoor.

Trap-Door Spiders and People

Trap-door spiders make their homes away from people. They don't live in buildings, as do many other kinds of spiders. They are extremely shy, and they stay hidden in their tunnels with the trapdoors closed tight if they know dangerous creatures, such as people, are nearby. Even scientists who are trained to spot trap-door spider tunnels can have trouble finding the tunnels. Trap-door spiders are not dangerous to humans, unless they bite someone who is allergic to spiders. People can be dangerous to trap-door spiders, though. Trap-door spiders need a certain type of **habitat** in which to live. If their habitat, such as a sunny hillside, is destroyed by new roads or new buildings, it can be hard for trap-door spiders to stay alive.

Glossary

abdomen (AB-duh-min) The large, rear section of an insect's or a spider's body.

camouflaged (KA-muh-flajd) Hidden by using a color and a pattern that matches one's surroundings.

cephalothorax (sef-uh-loh-THOR-aks) A spider's smaller, front body part, containing its head.

defense (DEE-fents) Something that saves from harm.

family (FAM-lee) The scientific name for a large group of plants or animals that are alike in some ways.

fangs (FANGZ) Hollow teeth that inject venom.

glands (GLANDZ) Organs or parts of the body that produce an element to help with bodily functions.

habitat (HA-bih-tat) The surroundings where an animal or a plant naturally lives.

mate (MAYT) To join together to make babies.

paralyze (PAR-uh-lyz) To lose feeling or movement in the limbs.

pheromones (FER-uh-mohnz) A kind of chemical produced by an animal that allows it to send a message to another of the same kind of animal.

predators (PREH-duh-terz) Animals that kill other animals for food.

prey (PRAY) An animal that is hunted by another animal for food.

species (SPEE-sheez) A single kind of plant or animal. All people are one species.

spinnerets (spih-nuh-RETS) Parts, located on the rear of the spider's body, that release silk.

venom (VEH-num) A poison passed by one animal into another through a bite or a sting.

Index

Web Sites

Due to the changing nature of Internet links, PowerKids Press has developed an online list of Web sites related to the subject of this book. This site is updated regularly. Please use this link to access the list:

www.powerkidslinks.com/lspi/trapdoor/